Contents

Confused? Get Started with Wedding Themes!

Chapter 1

First things first: there are lots of wedding theme ideas available. But sometimes, the number can work for your disadvantage and you can be lost with what particular theme to choose. The truth, however, is that choosing a wedding theme is simple. All you have to do is get at the right start and everything will follow easily.

So where to begin?

1. Begin by identifying your wedding date.

A date of your wedding says it all. For example, you have chosen to get married in summer, then go for a summer wedding theme or a beach wedding theme. If you want to get married during winter, then a Christmas or winter wedding theme is for you. And so on...

In other words, once you have identified your wedding date, it is easy for you to choose a wedding theme since there are just a limited number of themes that are suitable for a particular season.

Another good thing about starting off by identifying a wedding date is that you have a good head start in your wedding preparation. As we all know, a one day wedding affair takes a lot of time to prepare. Making sure that you have set the date early will also give you more time to think and gather everything you need that will fit the theme you have selected.

But what if you do not know when to hold your wedding? Another alternative is...

2. Begin by identifying your wedding venue.

If you decide to hold you wedding at a beach resort, you can easily use a beach wedding theme. If you want to get married at a farm or a ranch, then you can go for Western wedding thing. If you want the traditional church wedding, then you can add flavor to it by using one of the several wedding theme options like Victorian, Roman, Irish, or Romeo and Juliet.

The thing is, the wedding venue is a very good source of inspiration when choosing a wedding theme.

Aside from this, deciding the wedding venue early assures you that you have booked the venue for your wedding date. This is helpful since it is very difficult to have everything planned only to know that the venue you have selected is already booked.

3. Begin by knowing what you want.

This is another way to start if you have several things in mind. For example, if you want a fairy-tale-like wedding or if you want to ride a horse-drawn carriage, then there are several themes like the Cinderella wedding theme. If you like to get married oriental-inspired, then you can use the Chinese or Japanese wedding theme. If you want to get married in a unique theme, then come up with your own theme.

What you need here is the basic knowledge of what you want. This is your wedding and no one should be happier than you. Just think of what you want and the idea will come out easily.

Choosing a wedding theme is just the beginning. You have a lot of things to prepare. But the good thing is, once you have your wedding theme set, you already have the blueprint of your wedding which makes it easier for you to make a perfect theme wedding.

Deciding a Wedding Theme

Chapter 2

No matter where you are in the country, you will all agree that wedding is both an exciting and stressful event to plan. But there is a way to undo this belief: decide a wedding theme. This can certainly increase the excitement and lessen the stress since the theme will define everything you need for your wedding from dresses to the accessories; from cakes to the foods; and from invitation to location.

So how should you decide what wedding theme to choose?

Consider your personalities and interest. This is the best way to pull out a theme out of nothing. If you both love the sea, then consider a beach theme wedding.

If you both come from the West, then a Western and Country wedding theme will suit both of you.

If you have different cultural orientation, then why not pick one traditional wedding ceremony?

If one of you is from the military, then a military wedding would be impressive.

Or, if the bride likes fairy tales, then why not consider

a fairy tale wedding. This will certainly give another meaning to the word "happily ever after", right?

Wedding themes that are based on your favorite movie could be another idea you can consider.

NASCAR wedding theme can be a good choice too.

The fact is, there could be thousands of different wedding themes you can choose from. It is up to both of you to decide which one will describe yourselves best.

If you have, for example, made a list of different wedding themes but could not really pin point which to you choose, then consider the time of the wedding. Sometimes, it is good thing know first when to get married then decide which theme is perfect for that season. There are particular wedding themes during spring and summer, so as the winter and fall. If you want a wedding in December, then a Christmas wedding theme could be great. A February wedding is expected to have a Valentine's Day wedding theme.

The place where you will hold your wedding is also a good start to know which theme to choose. If it is a ranch, then a Country wedding theme is perfect. The beach wedding in Hawaii is of course not as good if you don't adapt the Hawaiian wedding theme. A garden wedding theme will obviously work if hold at the garden. Holding the wedding at the Disney World will automatically be a Disney wedding theme.

A period of history that both of you may want to highlight during your wedding is also a good start when deciding the theme you will use. Some of these are Renaissance wedding theme, Roman wedding theme, and Ancient China wedding theme.

Deciding a wedding theme early is one thing. Preparing for the things that will fit to the theme is another. So after you have decided which wedding theme to choose, your tasks are now on preparing the things needed for the wedding including the decorations, accessories, food, wedding dresses or costumes, invitations, and more. Make sure that everything is based on the theme.

Nonetheless, a defined wedding theme will make the preparation easier since the theme will set the limits of the things needed. The wedding theme will make the preparation into order at the same time, it will give a unique experience to those who will attend the celebration.

Choosing a Wedding Color Theme

Chapter 3

Reception, flowers, church, wedding dress, music, decorations, and wedding color. A daunting task indeed. But all you need is a bit of organization to accomplish all of these. Start right by choosing a wedding color theme.

Choosing a wedding color is simple. All you have to do is choose a primary color and secondary colors. Okay, it is still quite unclear to you how so here's what you should do to finally decide which color to choose.

Think of all the colors that appeal to you. List them down. You may probably have written several colors already.

Now, consider the time or season you are getting married. If it is winter, then dark colors such as burgundies and dark purples are perfect. For summer and spring wedding, bright colors such as yellow and orange good. Pastel colors fit as well. For Christmas themed wedding, green, silver, white or red can be used. Browns, reds, yellows, and burnt oranges are for fall wedding as they are the colors of the harvest time.

Pick the color from your list that matches the season of your wedding date.

Then, choose 2 secondary colors. It helps to look at the color wheel to know which colors match.

If you still find it difficult to choose the colors of your wedding, then you have 2 places to go: the wedding boutique and the ramp.

Look at flower arrangements to see which colors look great together. You can also ask for flower arrangers to suggest color combinations. Or, ask a clerk which colors come perfectly with the dress. The bridesmaids dress can also be a source of your wedding color.

Ramp suggests designs and colors straight from the designers. Okay, you don't have access to "fashion exhibitions". Look at magazines. You can definitely find unique and elegant wedding colors there.

Another place to find a good color combination is the butterfly garden, Why? You can never find the most amazing and inspiring color combinations anywhere in the world than from butterflies. Or, if there are no butterfly gardens near you, the encyclopedia will show you every single butterfly species known to man. Okay, no encyclopedia. Search the web. The point is, find inspiration from nature and you can surely pick up one instantly.

There are other ways to find a good color for your wedding. One of these is watching sports. Now, grooms will love this part. Search for the different color combinations of each team. Then, pick one that you are comfortable with.

There are also popular wedding color combinations you want to adapt. These are: soft pink and brown, pink and green, hot pink and black, fuschia and lime green, and fuschia and orange, blush and burgundy, silver & white, yellow and grey, blue and white, emerald green and gold.

Orange (Alstromeria, Chrysanthemum, Gerbera Daisy, Asiatic Lily, Snapdragons, and Zinnia)

Pink (Alstromeria, Chrysanthemum, Freesia, Gerbera Daisy, Hydrangea, Larkspur, Asiatic Lily, Oriental Lily, Lisianthus, Matsumoto Asters Snapdragons, Yarrow, and Zinnia)

Decorations and Accessories. Fine linens for tables and summer-themed materials for centerpieces are the usual choice. Use sand, water, seashells, fruits, and colors to bring out the summer theme you want to achieve.

Autumn Wedding Theme: Irony between Gloom and Celebration

Chapter 16

Probably not one of the typically chosen wedding themes but absolutely one that could be very appealing. Who would have thought of celebrating in the midst of underlying shades and shadows? But with a little creativity, you could always take advantage of the pleasure of celebrating your wedding amidst the falling leaves and the gloominess of the atmosphere.

But apart from the leaves that would renew in the coming days and the weather that would turn lighter in the next months, autumn is also marked with warmth and beauty that is beyond human expression.

Here are some suggestions for your autumn wedding theme:

Colors mark autumn wedding themes. Some of the best examples that you could use are those that could be found in the shades of nature itself during this season. The colors are normally characterized by rich and bold colors such as deep greens, gold, copper and creams, yellows, oranges and maroons and a couple of other shades that surround even the very reception wherein you would conduct your wedding ceremony. In fact, if you are to use an autumn wedding theme, you could take advantage of the natural setting the season projects. Such is the case of moderately arranged garden filled with fallen leaves and a spread of earth colors.

An autumn wedding theme would never be complete without the pumpkins. Why use flower vases if you could turn pumpkins into centerpieces?

Not only would an autumn wedding invitation accentuate your entire concept, it could also help set the mood for your wedding. There are several companies now that produce wedding invitations so be sure to check on any of them. However, if you are making your own wedding invitation, it would be a good idea to make use of elegant brown paper with embossed leaf or an image of leaves on top plus accents of gold and copper powder.

The ceremony doesn't necessarily have to follow the usual ones we could see in most weddings. Instead of making your flower girl drop petals of flowers, you could choose to use leaves for a change. A combination of choice leaves could add to the effects the fallen leaves in the grounds provide.

The costumes would also have to be in accordance with the theme. If you choose to use leaves as the primary object in all your wedding items, you must see the consistency in it. For example, your garland could be a mixture of leaves and flowers bonded around twigs and small branches.

The dress should also project the theme. It would be a good idea to look for something that is light with simple cuts yet projects a subtle elegance.

As for the males, you can always try something different without necessarily following the traditional wedding tuxedos. You adapt the fashion of the season and get something that could truly match your wedding theme.

Also, don't forget to use a shower of fire-colored leaves all over the place. You can buy artificial items from crafts shop or may collect natural leaves from chosen trees and plants. You could make use of some of the fruits and flowers commonly grown during this season.

Dreamy would describe an autumn wedding theme that could be emphasized by the choices of objects that are normally seen in an autumn setting. If your choices appeal to this kind of these, it would be best to plan your wedding during this season.

Winter Theme Wedding Ideas

Chapter 17

Although most of the wedding ceremonies are scheduled during Summer and Spring, no one will stop you if you decide to hold your wedding during the winter season. So if at this point you have decided to get married when the snow is falling and everyone is celebrating the holidays, then here are some winter theme wedding ideas for you:

Where to have a winter wedding?

Ski resort, a private club or a historic mansion can be some of your choices when you want a winter wedding atmosphere. But if you want a private wedding with few people invited, a house or inn with a fireplace can already make the ceremony intimate. That is of course if you live or want to hold your wedding at the state with a guaranteed snow during the date of your wedding.

If otherwise you live or plan to hold your wedding to place without snow but are still cold, then you have to add winter elements to the wedding to make it more winter-themed.

Tip: Make sure that the place where you plan to hold your wedding is adequately heated during the winter season, especially during your wedding date. Check if they use seasonal decorations as most places are already heavily decorated during this time of the year. This will save you money.

What to wear at the winter wedding?

Bride – It is always expected that a bride would wear a long silk gown during the wedding since wedding gowns are often designed to be worn during a temperate climate. The wedding gown suitable during the winter wedding should involve more capes, shrugs, wraps, and coats to protect the bride from cool temperature. Unless of course, you want to hold your wedding in an adequately heated room. The thing is, you have to adapt your dress to the venue of the wedding and the activities where you will do.

Groom – and groomsmen do not require special designs for their attire. A coat and long pants would be enough.

What to serve at the reception?

To get a winter theme wedding cakes, decorate with sugar sculptures, silver embellishments, or snowflake patterns. Special treats can include spiced wine, eggnog or hot chocolate. Ask your caterer to serve food that would be timely and would fit your wedding theme.

What flowers to use?

White and silver flowers are perfect for winter theme weddings. To celebrate the season, red and green can be used as well. White flowers include roses, crocus, stephanotis, lilies, and football mums. Silver flowers include baby blue eucalyptus, silver-dollar eucalyptus, and dusty miller. For less expensive flowers, there are roses, tulips, and ornamental berries, which grow during the winter season. Talk to your florist on what flowers you want to use.

What décors fit the winter wedding theme?

Any Christmas decorations like Christmas tree, mistletoe, etc. will do if you want to achieve the ambiance of winter. Do not invite Santa Claus and his reindeers though. Add some lighting effect around the room using pillars of candles arranged with white pillars. Use floating candles as a simple holiday centerpiece decorated with snowflake effects.

The thing is, there are probably thousands of ideas you can apply to your winter wedding. All you have to do is to use your imagination or ask your friends for contribution on what are the things that will truly make a winter wedding special.

Types of Cakes for Theme Weddings

Chapter 18

People are becoming obsessive with wedding themes these days. In fact, it would be almost unbelievable if a new couple would not use a theme for their wedding.

What's so fancy with wedding themes is that you could customize the look and sometimes even the nature of the ceremony itself. From wedding favors to dresses and cakes, you could select any theme and match each one of these to maximize the effects and feel of your special day.

It would be awkward if not all main components of your wedding would coordinate given the fact that you have selected your theme. Thus, our first recommendation is that you find the most fitting type of wedding cake with your wedding theme so that you would further actualize the loveliness of your selected motif.

In this article, we will just discuss three of the most common types of cakes used in most themed weddings.

Traditional wedding cakes

Wedding cakes are normally coated with an ivory icing and is characterized with a multi-layered cake design. The elegance of this type of cake is gathered from its pillars and icing. While this has been the trend since who-knows-when, we still could not negate the fact that the traditional designs could still bring out the best from a wedding theme, even those of the modern-like ones.

Victorian wedding themes mostly benefit from traditional cakes. With the elegance and grandeur of this wedding cake, Victorian tradition lovers would surely opt for a cake that could be typified with this era. One that displays luxury, majesty and sophistication.

Traditional wedding cake designs would also apply with flower wedding themes. Such cakes would be typically incorporated with flower and fruits designs instead of plain icing and candy flower decors.

Contemporary wedding cakes

This type of cakes opened new alleys for creating more adventurous and less traditional styles of cakes. In fact, with the continuous trend towards newer ideas in wedding, people have also in turn found new ways of creating and recreating wedding cakes through contemporary designs.

Typically, such designs would only apply for non-traditional wedding themes such as Disney land wedding theme or those of the fairyland wedding theme. When talking about contemporary designs, the list of types could be endless. From pillar to castle and even wonky cakes, you will find every single design a lot different from that of the other. When your wedding theme requires the use of non-tiered or ivory icing-laden wedding cake, you could always look at the option of using contemporary ideas for cakes.

The variations come from both the inner structure of the cake and the finishing touches. A single component removed could mean so much when it is added. For example, a moon shaped wedding might need a few touches that would further accentuate the entire result.

Alternative wedding cakes

Whenever someone says alternative cakes, the first thought that could come into your mind is a picture of an out of this world cake design that is not tied with normal perception of cakes but falls more into the category with experimental features.

This option is best for couples considering new concepts in relation to their wedding themes. Wedding themes such as country wedding, beach wedding, princess wedding and star wedding are among the most typical categories that fall into this type of wedding cake.

Autumn Wedding Theme: Irony between Gloom and Celebration

Probably not one of the typically chosen wedding themes but absolutely one that could be very appealing. Who would have thought of celebrating in the midst of underlying shades and shadows? But with a little creativity, you could always take advantage of the pleasure of celebrating your wedding amidst the falling leaves and the gloominess of the atmosphere.

But apart from the leaves that would renew in the coming days and the weather that would turn lighter in the next months, autumn is also marked with warmth and beauty that is beyond human expression.

In Closing...

There are unlimited design possibilities that exsist when it comes to wedding themes. Use your imagination, what atmosphere do you want to evoke? Make this once in a lifetime event really your own and showcase your personality and that of your groom!

If you have already chosen your wedding color, avoid accenting too much black. Though black is elegant and very formal, too much of it may look like a funeral.

Wrap up: There is no perfect wedding color; so you have the liberty to select among thousands of color shades. Make sure though that you are comfortable with your color choice even though your choices are not very popular. Choose the colors that will tell something about you as a couple and mood you want to achieve during your wedding. If your first color choice does not suit you, choose another. Do not stop until you are comfortable with your color choice.

Beach Theme Wedding Ideas

Chapter 4

Choosing a beach theme wedding gives you a lot of advantages. One is giving yourself the total freedom to become creative and making your wedding celebration a totally unique one. Depending on the time of the day, the nature can help you to achieve the mood you want to set. A mid summer-day is the time for celebration, party, activity, excitement, and fun. The dawn or dusk provides a romantic feel to the event.

And another good thing is: a beach wedding does not require a lot of decorations- the beach will serve as your backdrop.

Having said that, planning the perfect time of wedding is important. A big celebration is ideal during the mid-day where you can involve all of your guests with the fun. On the other hand, a small and private ceremony at the seaside with few guests is ideal to be held at dawn or dusk.

However, do not disregard beach theme wedding if do not have an access to an ocean. After all, a beach can be a river or a lake. Both can be very ideal venues for a beach theme wedding.

Nonetheless, you have to remember this: "There are no rules to follow!"

Do not contain your wedding preparation within the boundaries of the traditional wedding. Of course, the basic elements of the ceremony should not be omitted. But the rest, you can change. Be creative. Make it fun. Or rather, have fun. It is your day so maximize it by doing what you want to do.

Here are some wedding theme ideas you can use as a jumping point:

Caribbean wedding theme ideas –

You do not have to fly to the Caribbean to enjoy the infamous Caribbean-style wedding. All you have to do is to choose a good shoreline and add the missing ingredients: Wear the usual colored shirt, shorts, sarong or wrap. Ask your guests to wear such things as well. Leave your shoes at your car or your hotel room. Sip tropical drinks and punch rum all through the night. Dance with a reggae and calypso music. Add some tropical flowers. Play the "limbo rock". Prepare bamboo torches around the party area.

Hawaiian beach wedding ideas –

You don't have to watch "Lilo and Stitch" or "Blue Hawaii" to get the idea. Choose a white tops and shorts for the groom while a traditional Hawaiian gown called the "holoku" is for the bride. Ask your guests to wear colorful shirt or the Hawaiian shirt. Want to go further? Then consider the grass hula skirts. Do not forget the lei and haku. Shoes are definitely useless. Wear flip flops or go barefoot. The Hawaiian beach wedding is informal yet beautiful.

Fantasy wedding theme ideas –

Any women would not forget to live their dreams to become a princess. Now, here is your chance. The bride can become Cinderella and the groom prince charming. Arrive at the venue with a horse-drawn carriage. Make a sand castle as your background. Make a costume also for the bridesmaid and the groomsmen.

Thankfully, Shrek was not yet created during your childhood fantasies. It saves you from transporting a donkey at your wedding.

Beach party wedding theme ideas –

If you want cheap, stress-free, and informal celebration, this one's for you. Let loose with just shorts and simple dress. Ask your guests to bring their own swimwear. Make it like a unique family outing with barbeque and beach volleyball.

Essential Elements in Beach Theme Wedding

Chapter 5

So you have decided to go for a beach theme wedding. Your next task is to gather all the things needed that suite the beach wedding theme you want to achieve. To help you on this, here are the essential elements that you can go without:

Groom's Attire. The key to a good groom's attire, which is also applicable to all those people who will come, is wearing casuals. Khaki pants and a white long-sleeve polo and simple yet elegant to wear. Or, a Hawaiian shirt would do, matched with beige short pants. The groom can also wear white tops and white pants. This will not only match the theme of your wedding, it will also keep the ceremony less formal and more fun than the conventional church wedding.

Groomsmen's Attire. The groomsmen often wear clothes similar to the groom although they can always let lose on what to wear since it is a beach wedding. You get the point.

Bride's Attire. A simple white gown is always the best choice for the bride. To make it more beach themed-attire, wear a tropical flower or flower wreaths to your hair.

Bridesmaids' Attire. Clothes that match your wedding color

scheme are always a great choice as the bridesmaids' attire.

Footwear. Flip flops are enough to match theme but if you want to feel the sand on your feet, then no one is stopping you to go barefooted. After all, you can save money doing it since you don't have to buy new shoes.

Wedding Invitation. An invitation always creates the first impression to any occasion. So, if you want to emphasize your wedding theme, make beach wedding motif invitations. You have probably heard of an invitation inserted inside a bottle or an invitation with a printed picture of a tropical beach. Be creative and conceptualize your wedding invitation carefully.

Centerpieces. Candles surrounded by seashells and decorated by confetti and white sand can create a good centerpiece for your beach theme wedding. You can also go for a tall fishbowl half-filled with white sand and decorated with sea flowers or corals on the top.

Wedding Favors. There are lots of beach theme wedding favors available at any novelty shops. Some of the choices are: Flip flops keychain, scallop shell keychain, miniature tin pale decorated with seashells with candles, handcrafted wooden sails, seashell place card holder, beach-themed art coaster, beach chair place card holder, shell bookmarks, and more. Just choose from these or create one of your own.

Decorations. There are lots of inexpensive materials that will work well as decorations for your beach wedding. There are: Pearls, seashell of various shapes and sizes, star fish, beach sand, anchors, drift woods, nets, rope, oars, life rings, beach balls, buoys, and surfing boards. Use some of these materials which you think are appropriate and will bring out a beach wedding atmosphere. Or, use the beach as your background. The nature itself will give definition to your beach theme wedding.

Wedding reception. A beach theme wedding is best if both the ceremony and the reception are held at the beach. Here, you can just add simple decorations on and around the tables and chairs since you already have the sea, sand, and waves around you.

One important thing though: avoid overdoing all these elements. Instead, keep it simple yet elegant.

Go Back in Time with a Country Theme Wedding

Chapter 6

Relaxation, peace celebration...

These and everything else in between are the main dishes when you choose to have a country theme wedding.

If you and your couple would want to savor the starting moments of your lives together in simplicity and serenity, there is nothing that could answer these needs more than having it by going back through time in a laid back country scene.

Your idea of celebration would not be disturbed though. You could still throw a big party and allow your guests and family to enjoy the wedding celebration without having to risk yourselves against the prospect of going bizarre.

It may be an unusual idea to have your wedding in rustic charm but it is nevertheless a good option for those couples who have come to orient themselves with peace. Additionally, country wedding themes could best help transport you in a time when everything was simple and still.

Good locations for a country wedding theme are gracious country churches or inns, an elegant farmhouse, a barn, and places that reminisce the old good times.

You must be very choosy of your location though. A lovely farm-house in summer could not be as lovely in winter. In fact, you might even run the risk of having a miserable farmhouse amidst the chilly air and the looming possibility of snowfall. If you are planning to have a night wedding, however, you must seek the help of barn lanterns specially made for your wedding to project the feeling of bliss and placid atmosphere.

It would be best to wear something informal during your wedding. Allow yourself with comfortable white dresses that will let the breeze pass through. It would be a good scene to have your loose-fitting dress flow with the wind. A countryside groom, however, could wear an informal suit that is matched with a string tie. To give emphasis on a country wedding theme, you could use wild flowers as boutonnieres. The same concept must be used with the bridal party and the groom's men.

Each season matches its own country wedding theme. But, the most ideal season you could choose when planning to use the ideas covered by this theme is the spring and the summer. With these, you are more secured of the type of weather you would be anticipating.

Also, only in these seasons would you witness a plethora of floras and faunas. The butterflies and other lovely insects could invite themselves into your wedding reception or ceremony and add to the lovely guests you have gathered. Straws would also be great additions to your decors including the flowers that are abundant during these times of the year.

In fall, you could take advantage of the abundance of fiery-col-ored fallen leaves, dried corn and pumpkin. And for winter, why

not go for a cozy appeal? It would be romantic to set your ceremony in a great inn with a great hearth. On top of this atmosphere, why not hang perfect winter decors like boughs and holly?

Doing something unusual is one thing you could cherish all your
life. Country wedding themes would not only give you that special feeling but would also fill each of your second's worth with
wonderful memories of the biggest day of your life. And so, as you
walk the golden mile, seek the good old fashion air and dance to
its silent music for eternity.

Ideas You Can Use in Putting Up a Fall Wedding Theme

Chapter 7

Thinking that it is awkward to celebrate your wedding in fall? Think again.

In fact, fall is the season that intimacy is most likely to arise. It is also the period when everyone just want to come home and spend more time with their families. You could take advantage of these two factors when considering the season for your wedding. In the following years, all you would want is the communion of everyone to celebrate with you the wedding you had several years past.

Fall is among the best seasons of the year for wedding. While the weather could not be exactly predicted, it would still be nice that you have wedded on a date when the fiery-colored leaves have fallen and everything is prepared for a long calm sleep in winter.

Fall wedding decors

The first thing you would want to do is to set the mood for your fall wedding theme. There are many options to answer this need. For example, you could hang lavish decorations using rich and bold fall colors such as red, orange, brown, or yellow. However, a more modern approach is to use dark chocolate shades with accents of beige or royal blue. This could really create good affects that would suit the entire theme and the season itself.

Fall wedding venue

One of the most common problem couples have is the venue of the wedding. If you are using a fall wedding theme, your best options would be an 18th century place, a vineyard, an apple orchard or an inn. In fact, any place that could help you settle with the fall foliage could be a good option.

Fall wedding flowers

Flowers could never go out of the norm in any wedding theme. Fall flowers are most likely composed of roses, mums, yarrow, and daisies including a rich blend of fall leaves. Each of these could be combined to provide the warmth that is characterized with the season.

Fall wedding attire

A selection of cream, off-white or even brown and green shades could be used as the main color for your wedding dress. Bridesmaids could look best with jeweltone attires while men could wear color shades that match the color of those worn by females.

A fall wedding theme doesn't only suggest the use of colors that are typically linked with the season. You could also use various costume designs that would explore more into the meanings of the autumn season itself. You don't have to stick with conventional attires. Instead, you could use into the design of your clothes some resemblance of those worn by fairies. This would not only make a difference but would also create a whole new perspective of fall wedding theme.

Fall wedding cake

You don't have to follow the traditional sense of wedding cakes where ivory is the main color and everything else is text booked.

You could always experiment on some new flavors of cakes and newer designs. Fall wedding cakes could take a form of anything that is related with fall, say a red-brown leaf. Yet, it could also be that you remove the wedding cake and replace it with a pumpkin, apple or any types of pies and breads.

Fall wedding favors

There are endless lists for wedding favors during this season. Among the most common are the pumpkin-inspired ones and anything related with fallen leaves. You can even provide your guest with a cake or two of your favorite fall bread or cake recipe.

Italian Wedding Theme: A Focus on Italian Foods

Chapter 8

Thinking of celebrating your wedding with an Italian theme? Good. But then, you must understand that the main thing you should be worrying about, aside from the seams of your gown and the folds of the envelope for your invitation is the main chef that would be supervising the menu for the reception.

While each culture boasts an individual approach towards wedding, the Italians give their best with their specialties on food. And you must focus on food indeed!

It is not simply serving Italian foods but serve them with great pride and extensive pleasure. If you haven't attended an Italian wedding yet, it would do you good to hear that there are some celebrations that boast a 14-course meal.

If you appeal towards a traditional Italian theme wedding, you can trim down your meal into five or seven courses. Be sure though that you incorporate some of the best foods Italian culture offers.

Begin with a main course of beef or chicken. You can substitute this though with a meal of special Italian sausage. Side dishes could then be a mixture of delectable array of pastas, vegetable dishes, various meals presenting Italian cheeses and antipasto. It would also be best to offer a selection of fruits on your table such as plump grapes, kiwi, sweet pineapple, strawberries and others. An air of aromatic Italian breads must also be constantly sent through the air.

An Italian wedding cake is typically made of several grand layers that present two miniature figures of a bride and groom on top of the highest layer. While the cake is served with a superb coffee, it is not intended to be the only sweet thing in the meal. You could also offer a sweet blend of cookies and sweet breads that are thought to bring good luck for the new couple.

With fine food come some good drinks. Italians are good patrons of wines. On your wedding, assure to it that a choice of excellent wines is kept at hand to be offered to your guests through the entire ceremony.

The main disadvantage point of an Italian wedding theme is the inability of the couple to recreate the entire ceremony. Unlike some wedding themes, the couples have the discretion of re-making some of the components. In an Italian wedding theme however, you could only stick true with a Roman Catholic mass. Nevertheless, you could take advantage of the ceremony in the wedding reception. Let your guests dance the night away into superb selection of Italian music by classical composers and singers. Be careful also to include some festive songs that are typical with traditional Italian weddings.

As for your wedding dress, be keen to stick with only two colors: either pure white or ivory. Italians still stick with this traditional and there is no sign of ever changing the way things re being handled.

A silk white gown with its long train is perfect for a wedding dress. A veil is also of great importance. A bride normally wears this veil until the moment the priest announces for the groom to kiss the bride. This symbolizes purity and virginity. The veil itself symbolizes that the bride has never seen a man before.

A small satin bag is also integral for the entire ceremony. The bride has to hold this through out the celebration to stash the envelopes the guests would hand her.

An Italian wedding would never be complete without some favors to be given to the guests. The couple must secure some lovely assortment of candy-coated almonds wrapped in beautiful packages.

Las Vegas Theme Wedding: Breaking Grounds with New Options

Chapter 9

And so you fell in love with the Sin City…and found the lady or the man of your dreams? Why not celebrate your wedding in the city that brought you together?

It is a common notion to get married in Las Vegas style! Whether you want to tie the knot in the city itself or celebrate it somewhere else by recreating the place and turning it into a Nevada city, all you need to have are some handy ideas.

Of course, it would be far too different if you are to conduct the ceremony in Las Vegas and in a venue you have recreated. Thus your best choice is to fly to the Sin City and get wed.

There are so many chapels in Las Vegas that you could choose from. In fact, the place has already become synonymous with weddings. No wonder, there are a couple of companies specializing in Las Vegas theme weddings starting from the reception to wedding gowns and other things you should be worrying about.

While some hands could help you, it would still be ideal if you are going to plan for your wedding and follow the plans you have conceptualized. Probably, you might need some assistance with booking the venue and other external concerns yet you must personally deal with your wedding details to make it more meaningful and one that is worth keeping in your memories.

To start with, you must decide the colors of your theme and begin building the concepts from there. Common colors that work well with this wedding theme are red, white and black. However, you must not limit yourself with this selection. How about more experimental choices? Try something different, pastel colors may not be that too popular yet they would undeniably create a difference in design and effects.

There are various locations in Las Vegas that could affect your choice of a general concept of a theme. You don't have to follow what other people have already done. If you are going to get married in a church or chapel, you might want to wear the traditional white wedding dress and the formal tuxedo. But since you have a plethora of locations to choose from, you can start picking up some ideas for attires and costumes from the particular venue wherein you would conduct the ceremony and reception.

One that is truly popular in a Las Vegas theme wedding is the use of playing cards. Well, if you are fond of card games or you have already decided to incorporate this component into your theme then why not use them and maximize their use in the entire ceremony and throughout the reception?

However, you must not limit the scope of your idea with this typical notion. As we have stated earlier, you could use some new concepts. Again, don't be afraid of the process. Your new concepts might not initially appeal to your guest or to your family perhaps yet so long that they work well with your plans then why not recreate the general design of Las Vegas wedding.

However, if you are to celebrate your wedding reception in a casino, your best bet for a Las Vegas wedding theme is something that would be formal and sophisticated with the elements of a true Las Vegas wedding- cards, dice and gambling games.

Princess Wedding Theme: A True Display of Royalty

Chapter 10

Arrange every detail of your wedding as to fit for royalty.

One of the most common wedding themes nowadays is the realization of a girl's dream. Most ladies during their childhood dreamt of having her own castle, a wardrobe of magnificently created royal gowns, a crown that signifies her royalty, and a luscious garden wherein she could continue her wishful dreaming.

On your wedding day, why not live her dreams into reality?

While most would wish for a royal princess wedding, too few could truly throw such an event since there are needs for extravagant spending. Remember that without the touch of royalty and opulence, your princess wedding will never look real.

Your reception will greatly matter in this kind of wedding. If you can afford to rent a historic castle complete with luscious and carefully manicured lawn then well and good. But if this is too ambitious and very unaffordable, the next best thing would be a grand ballroom hall with high ceilings, an impressive staircase, awesome chandeliers and a long, red carpet to walk on during your entrance into the ceremony.

And since it is every girl's dream to look like a princess, you must answer this through furnishing a traditional ball wedding gown. This must be made with a full skirt and a fitted bodice that truly appeals to a princess-like royalty. Grace the gown with a fine detail of lace, pearls and other decorations. Your excellent choice of a train is the cathedral as this possesses splendor which must be carried by members of the wedding party. Also, select a diamond tiara with a long trail of veil to add to the air of luxury. Match this with a pair or carefully selected elbow-length gloves.

The bridesmaids must also be dressed in floor-length gowns that would much a fairytale's image of ladies in royal attendance. Richly colored satin dresses with fine addition of gloves and bouquets of flowers will help give more emphasis on a princess theme wedding.

To help set your guests' mood, you can make use of a hand-made paper invitation with a colored wax seal that posses your initials to secure the envelopes. The programs, however, must be made with engraved letters as well. This could best be rolled and tied as to resemble a royal invitation from the renaissance period.

Seal the air of a princess theme wedding with a royal dance through the music of classical composers, especially those who have focused on court waltz. It would be best to play music through the entire reception. However, it would still be best if you allot a budget for a string quartet. Like the princes and princesses of old age, you can reminisce your wedding by remembering how the guests looked upon you on your first graceful waltz. After which, allow your guests to take pleasure in the royalty you have set before them. Arrange the program of your wedding reception in a way that everyone could enjoy the night away through music and food.

End your night with a glorious exit. Hire a horse-drawn carriage and a tuxedo-clad driver to carry you towards your honeymoon venue.

Years after your wedding, you will find pleasure in looking back to the day you have lived out the very wishes you have dreamt since your childhood.

So You are Thinking of a Garden Theme Wedding

Chapter 11

So, your fiancé has already proposed for marriage. Yes, the one big day you have waited all your life for. And now, thoughts are flooding your mind.

Who's going to witness your wedding? What will be your wedding gown? What will be the general décor of the celebration? Where would you celebrate it?

These questions would most likely need careful pondering and planning. If you want to trim down your problem towards a specific concern, you should begin with choosing your wedding theme.

Wedding theme would provide the carefully selected and sometimes pre-determined motif of both the ceremony and the reception. This way, you will no longer have to run the risk of non-coordinated wedding plans. Well, you can always save yourself the trouble of planning through hiring professional wedding planners. But, wouldn't it be nicer if after years of marriage, you will look back to your wedding day and bear with pride that you were the brains behind your big day?

One of the most common wedding themes that used these days

is the garden wedding theme. Most couples opting for this option are those with common denominators such as love for serenity and simplicity, appreciation of certain romantic occurrences such as the blooming of the flowers and the sunrise and sunset.

Not that garden theme wedding is limited to people with these attitude. But it is just to give you the general idea of what a garden wedding theme.

So long as there is a lovely garden and some people to organize a wedding, there will always be a garden wedding that would be celebrated. Traditional and modern approaches towards garden theme wedding could be used.

There are endless options for garden wedding theme. If you know someone who has a lovely garden, you could ask him or her to organize the wedding with you. But to save you from some troubles, you could always rent a botanical garden, any rented lakeside location or any establishment that prides itself for its collection of natural beauty. Remember to book your location months before your wedding so as to ensure the availability of the place and the coordination of the entire plan itself.

Garden wedding colors are not among the major things you should be thinking about. Since gardens basically have a shower of various hues, you could always take advantage of the splash of colors in a way that it would enhance the motif of your wedding.

Traditional wedding dresses are usually made out from shades of white or cream. However, you also have the option of choosing any color for a change. Ensure, however, that your choices of colors would maximize the over-all garden wedding theme. Any fabric could be used though yet breezy fabric would best suit anytime of the day.

Also consider that it would be more romantic if you would not be wearing any footwear on your wedding day. However, compensate this with the subtle grandeur of the wedding dress. A simplistic approach could best do this with touches of elegance on the general cut and designs of the wedding dress.

Other concerns could be wedding favors, invitations, table arrangements, back drops, pillars, flower arrangements and food. In any part of your wedding theme, be sure to integrate some of the most natural components you witness occurring in a garden.

Spring Wedding Theme: A Perfect Idea for Your Wedding

Chapter 12

There are only four seasons in our part of the world. If you are planning to get married, then you have to choose the best one for your concept.

Winter appeals to lots of couples and so do autumn. Summer has also become a hit but you see, the most favorite since time immemorial has always been the spring.

No need for further introduction on how beautiful spring is, after all we have already witnessed the magnificence this season could provide.

So, what is our idea of a spring theme wedding?

The first thing you would want to do is decide what features this season you would most likely take advantage of. Then build your general and specific concepts from there. Here, we will help you discover the pointers you have if you choose a spring theme wedding.

When are you planning to have your spring wedding?

Well, there is much to see during spring and many of us have our own favorites. Each phase of the season has its own advantages and disadvantages. So begin your planning with picking the exact time of the season you would want to get married.

Do you love the budding of the flowers amidst the floral abundance or are you more like of the sunshine-after-winter personality? Or would you rather have it later during the season when the summer is about to close in? There are far too many wonders this time of the year could give and each wonder would help you give more emphasis on the occurrences surrounding you and the event you have waited all your life for.

It would be a great idea to get in time with the Easter season if you are to be married in the church. Or, if you are opting for a more traditional look, you must book your tuxedo and gowns in advance before the high school prom gets in.

What do you want to wear?

Couples getting married during this season are more likely to wear the usual dresses, gowns and tuxedos we see year round. This is because spring calls for not so rigid-looking attires and not so soft-looking ones. It's just right around the middle.

Something that is breezy and light and very versatile would be perfect for a spring wedding theme. You can have a sleeveless top with balloon skirt matched with a wrap to keep you warm in case the weather becomes chilly. See to it that your bridesmaids and other attendees are also provided with dresses that provide the same comfort. Remember that the weather could be very dodgy with being so hot or cold.

Moreover, there are too little issues when it comes to colors. But typically, brides are looking for more vibrant ones that project the hues of the season.

Get around the idea of using pastel colors though since this is becoming dreadfully and overly popular. A splash of colors from your guests would also be a good option. Allow your bridesmaids to choose their own colors and the groomsmen their own choice of tuxedos. Just be reminded though that all must have something that would coordinate them. There would be nothing wrong in not following the spring wedding theme entirely because by doing so, you will be keeping the air of diversity alive.

Tips on Putting Up a Victorian Theme Wedding

Chapter 13

Planning a Victorian-themed wedding is something that requires careful preparation and the willingness to shed money. Since you would need the bygone days factors, you must also be careful with your choices of ideas to follow your decorations, attires, favors, invitations and others with.

In this article, you will find some useful tips to help you set the Victorian mood on your big day.

Choose between over-all Victorian theme or mere resemblance of the Victorian era

First and foremost, you must decide if you are going to go all out or you will just choose certain elements in your wedding that would match with a Victorian wedding theme. For example, you could use the theme with your attire but not in the decors of the reception area. But of course, it could still be better if you'll incorporate the theme into each component of your wedding. But this would call for some good investments since you will have to rent or buy the components you would be using. Say accessories from this particular era.

Choose the wedding venue

Remember that among the biggest factors towards the achievement of a true Victorian theme wedding is the place of the ceremony and reception. The best option you must look into is an actual Victorian house or inn where the spirit of the era is left for preservation and eternal existence. But in the absence of this, you could always look for a Victorian inspired inn or a chair marked with Victorian classic styling. You could also consider a garden as your reception only ensures that this would be accessorized with plant arrangements and garden designs typical with this period.

Ensure also that there is a grand chandelier to witness your wedding day. Without this, your wedding would never be Victorian. But, if you prefer not to use a chandelier or two, you might look into the option of setting luxurious candelabras for a more casual look.

Choose your wedding attire

Victorian styled-wedding gown have always been pure white with high neck and long sleeves. This style is elegant indeed when combined with a pair of lace gloves and a sixpence in the shoe. Keep jewelries into their barest but don't forget to add a brooch at the neck or a veiled hat to keep with the Victorian flavor.

The groom would look best with a cutaway tuxedo and exceptionally large boutonnieres. You can also ask your guests to wear something Victorian in style. To keep the flavor oozing, we suggest that some of the pictures be made black and white.

Choose your wedding cake

Intend that your wedding cake be elaborately designed and majestic. An imposing image of a cake would surely accentuate the whole theme. Orange blossoms have always been a favorite topping but of course you could look for newer flavors that would emphasize the merging of one tradition with that of another.

Choose your wedding favor

Rosemary is among the most favorite Victorian wedding favor. This could be delivered in so many ways so long as the basic feature is the rosemary. Victorian frames and teacups would also be chic choices for a Victorian wedding favor.

What's so nice with this theme is that you could let your imagination play with the possibilities presented by the era. A little research will help you see more of the possibilities.

Tropical Theme Wedding: A New Look at Wedding Celebrations

Chapter 14

The warm breeze, the damp sea wind, the magnificence of the seashore, these surely are great splendors only found in the tropics.

No wonder, there are too many coupes wishing they could throw an excellent wedding celebration amidst the tropic's uniqueness.

Romance…spelled with a capital R! That's what a tropical theme wedding is. No more, no less.

How about doing a sunset wedding ceremony? Or do it as the sun rises perhaps? How lovely it would be for the groom to see tears from his bride's eyes painted with the colors of the sky during the sunrise. Or, the bride seeing the joy radiating from his partner's aura amidst the roaring surf of the sea and the back drop of colors from morning sun.

From the strands of hair driven to air by the wind or the little creatures that crawl the shore. The air of the celebration and the festive feeling seen from everyone's face. Everything about a tropical theme wedding is utterly romantic. So why not make one yourself?

There are simply lots of ways to fashion your tropical wedding theme. The trick though lies in the subtle simplicity behind the elegance of each wedding celebration.

You could go anywhere from wacky to formal when following a tropical wedding theme. You could choose to wear Hawaiian tops and downs or stylish bridal gown and tuxedos. There are no boundaries so long as you love the way you want to deal with your wedding theme.

Furthermore, a tropical wedding theme is something that you would go after when all you want is to strengthen the foundation of your family ties. There are no specially strict rules when celebrating it and it could give you no hassle when it comes to attending to all the people involved. This is true since the tropical atmosphere only calls for a free flowing reception, easy going attitude and carefree approach towards everyone and everything involved.

It is, over all, a new approach on wedding and extra emphasis on honeymoon. In fact, tropical theme weddings are more likely celebrated in honeymoon destinations and are more or less very intimate affairs. For those who are more comfortable sharing their big day with closely knit family and friends, this type of wedding might serve you best rather than throwing a grand, formal celebration.

Whether you bring all your guests in a special destination or celebrate in a local beach resort, it really doesn't matter. It's all about the way you carry things to win them over your side. Also, there is not much to bother in terms of clothes and the venue itself since the more simple it gets, the closer you approach the elegance with simplistic approaches.

You can have your bridesmaid wear breezy dresses that would

help them move a lot easier rather than giving them stiff clothes that are typical with cathedral weddings. The groomsmen could, in turn, wear beach attires or semi formal tuxedos depending on the general theme of the wedding.

But really, with a tropical wedding theme you can get the best for less without having to follow unbending traditions and unnecessary rules by following your own notions and ideas of what a wedding must appear like.

Want a romantic wedding celebration in style and simplicity? You must really go for a tropical wedding theme.

What Makes a Perfect Summer Theme Wedding

Chapter 15

Wedding dress and wedding color, music, food and reception, invitations and venue, flowers, decoration and accessories- All these and more must be prepared for your wedding. And if you are not ready enough, any small mishap on one can put a big dent on your whole wedding celebration. But surely, you don't want that to happen so you will try your best to make it perfect, especially if your wedding is in summer and your theme, summer. But makes a summer theme wedding perfect?

To answer this question, you don't have to go too far. All you have to do is to make sure that the elements in your wedding are given enough attention to details.

Wedding dress and wedding color. Summer always signifies the sun. So there is no better way to associate summer to your wedding than by looking at the nature and seeing the effects of the sun to it. Your wedding dress should be fitted to the heat. A soft silk white dress always gives beauty to the bride during summer wedding. Bright colors like oranges, yellows and reds that are often associated with harvest are some of the good choices of wedding color.

Music. Choosing music that celebrates your wedding, at the same time, suitable to the season should be your focus. Since summer is time to celebrate the sun, then make it more of a real celebration with dance and fast-beat music.

Food and reception. The summer is the season where most tropical fruits grow so don't forget to add a tropical flavor to your food. This applies whether you are holding your wedding reception at a beach resort or a restaurant. Speaking of reception, the most popular places where you can hold your summer theme wedding are the Caribbean, Hawaii and any tropical country or state where you can feel the heat of the sun. A beach resort is always a great choice.

Invitation and venue. To make your invitation a genuinely summer-themed, then go for the elements that often symbolize it. Sand, seashell, and other related things are enough to highlight your wedding theme. Since invitation gives the guest the first impression and the idea of what to expect on your wedding, it is recommended that you make one that will capture your whole wedding theme. Popular venues for summer theme wedding are the beach, garden, camping sites, and of course, the church. Choose one that you think is the best for your wedding.

Flowers. One of the most difficult decisions to make in your entire wedding preparation is choosing the flowers. Here are some of flowers that bloom during this season according to color:

White (Chrysanthemum, Freesia, Gerbera Daisy, Hydrangea, Iris, Larkspur, Lily Asiatic, Lily oriental, Lisianthus, Monte Casino Asters, Queen Anne's Lace, Snapdragons, Stephanotis, Stock, and Tuberose).

Yellow (Alstromeria, Chrysanthemum, Freesia, Gerbera Daisy, Lily, Asiatic, Snapdragons, Solidago, Sunflower, and Yarrow)